BEST OF

ADELE

2ND EDITION

BIG-NOTE PIANO

ISBN 978-1-70516-098-5

HAL•LEONARD®

Visit Hal Leonard Online at
www.halleonard.com

Contact us:
Hal Leonard
7777 West Bluemound Road
Milwaukee, WI 53213
Email: info@halleonard.com

In Europe, contact:
Hal Leonard Europe Limited
42 Wigmore Street
Marylebone, London, W1U 2RN
Email: info@halleonardeurope.com

In Australia, contact:
Hal Leonard Australia Pty. Ltd.
4 Lentara Court
Cheltenham, Victoria, 3192 Australia
Email: info@halleonard.com.au

CONTENTS

CHASING PAVEMENTS

Words and Music by ADELE ADKINS
and FRANCIS EG WHITE

I tell the world, ___ I'll
build my-self up _____ and

nev - er say e - nough, 'cause it was
fly a - round in cir - cles, wait - ing

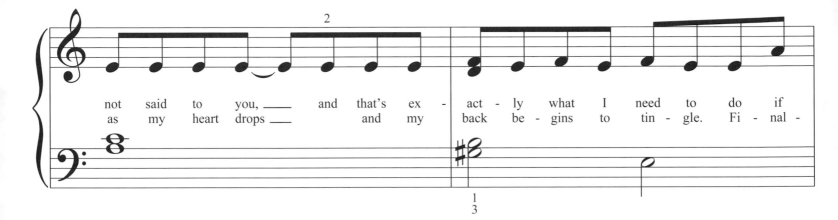

not said to you, ___ and that's ex -
as my heart drops ___ and my

act - ly what I need to do if
back be - gins to tin - gle. Fi - nal -

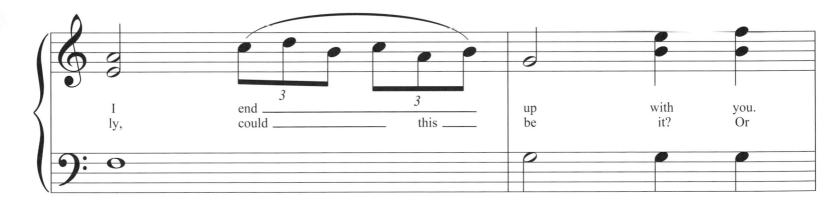

I end _____ this ___
ly, could _____ this ___

up with you.
be with it? Or

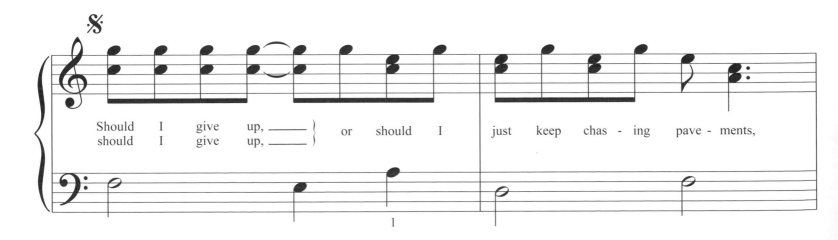

Should I give up, _____ or should I
should I give up, _____

just keep chas - ing pave - ments,

e - ven if it leads no - where? _____ Or would it be a waste e - ven

if I knew my place? Should I leave it there? _____

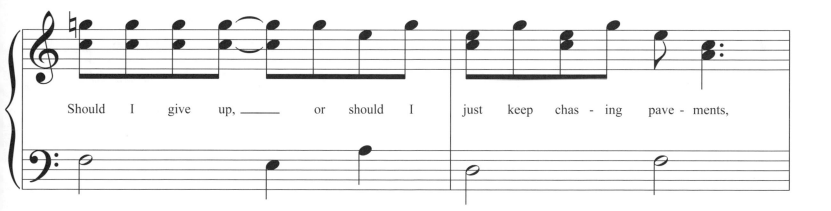

Should I give up, _____ or should I just keep chas - ing pave - ments,

To Coda ⊕ | 1.

e - ven if it leads no - where? _____ I

6

leads no - where? _____ Yeah. _____

4

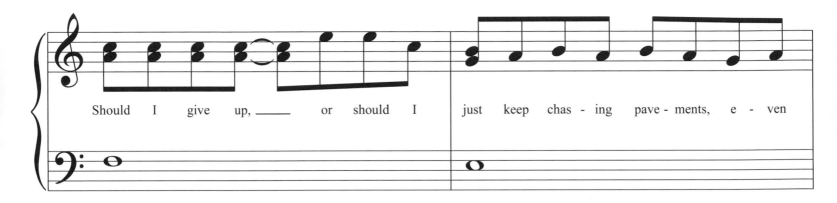

Should I give up, _____ or should I just keep chas - ing pave - ments, e - ven

if it leads no - where? _ Or would it be a waste e - ven if I

knew my place? Should I leave it there? _____ Should I _____

give up, _____ or should I just keep _ on _____ chas - ing _____

_____ pave - ments? _ Should I just keep _ on _____ chas - ing

D.S. al Coda

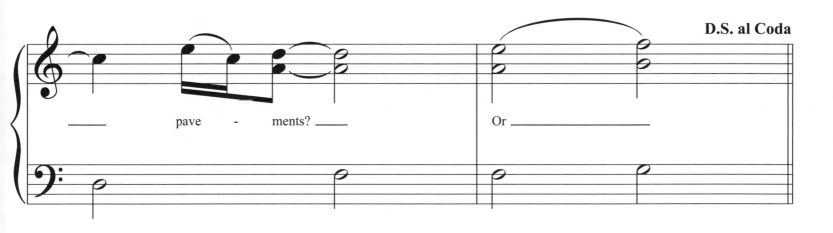

_____ pave - ments? _____ Or _____

CODA

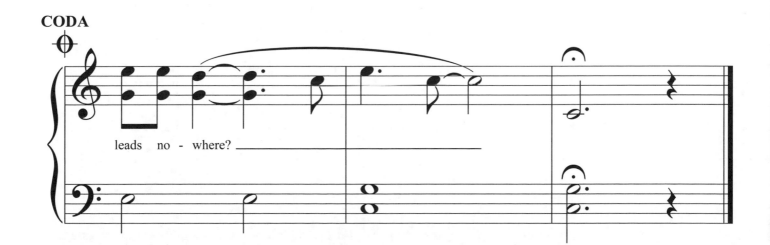

leads no - where? _____

HOLD ON

Words and Music by ADELE ADKINS
and DEAN JOSIAH COVER

Medium Gospel

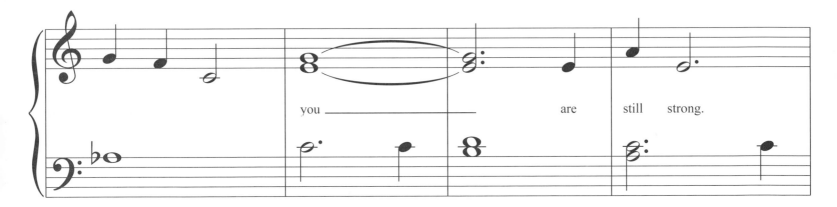

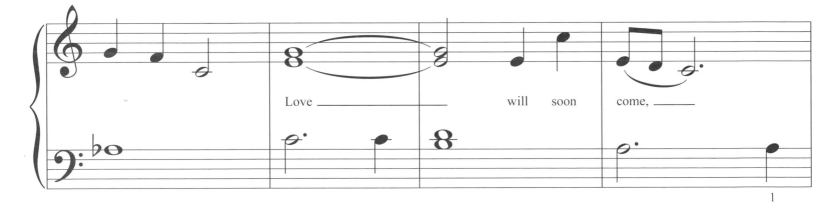

just hold, _____ hold on. _____

mf Oh, what have ____ I done, yet _____ a - gain?

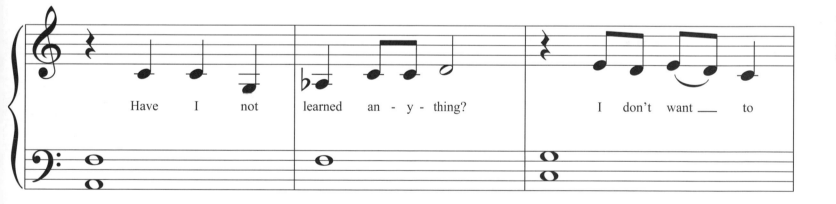

Have I not learned an - y - thing? I don't want ____ to

live in cha - os, it's like a ride that I want to get off.

It's hard to hold on - to _____ who I am when I'm stum - bling in the

dark for a hand. I am so tired _____ of bat - tling _____

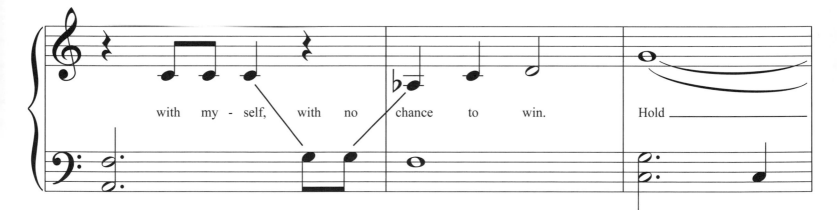

with my - self, with no chance to win. Hold _____

_____ on, let time be pa - tient,

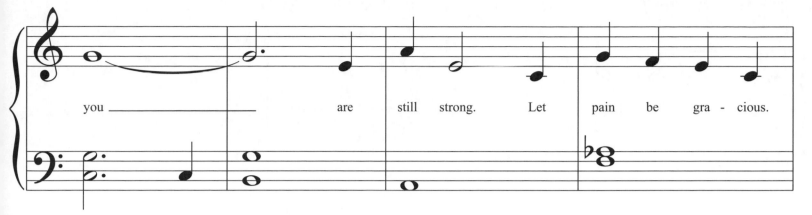

you _____ are still strong. Let pain be gra - cious.

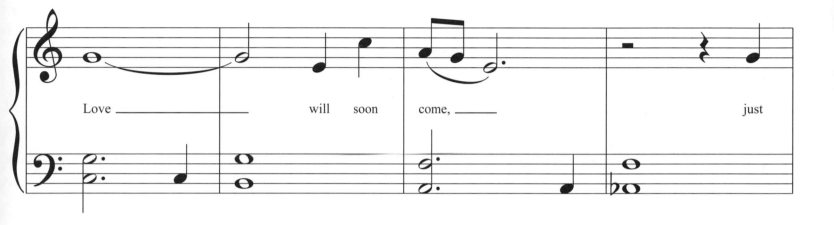

Love _____ will soon come, _____ just

hold, _____ hold on. _____

I swear to God, I am such a mess, the hard - er that I

try, I re - gress. I'm ___ my own worst en - e - my,

right now I tru - ly hate be - ing me. Ev - 'ry day feels

like the road I'm on might just o - pen up and swal - low me whole.

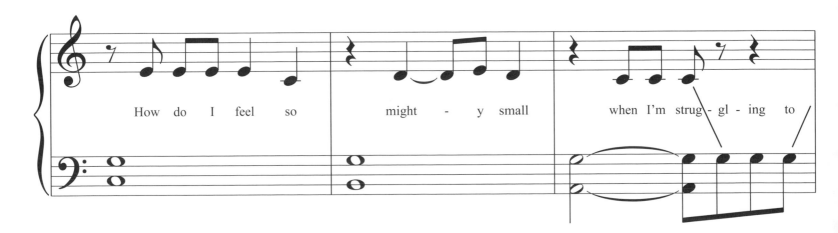

How do I feel so might - y small when I'm strug - gl - ing to

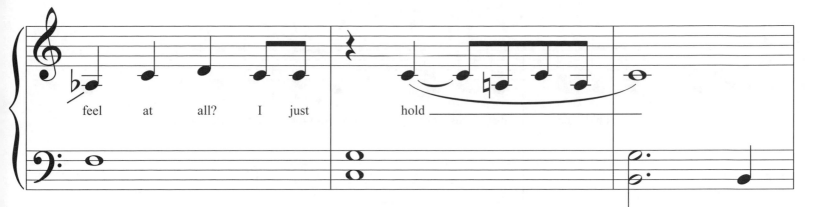

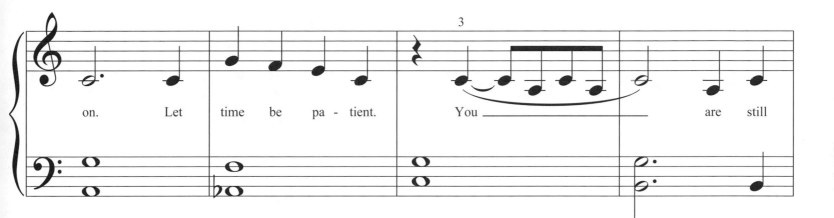

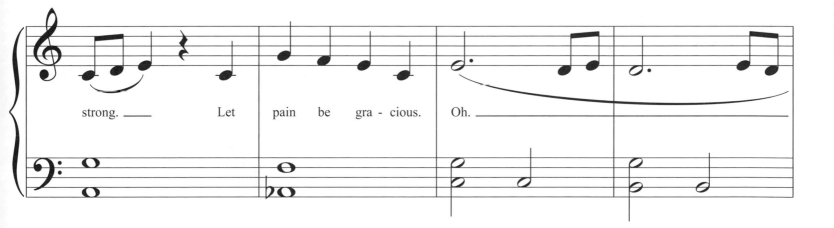

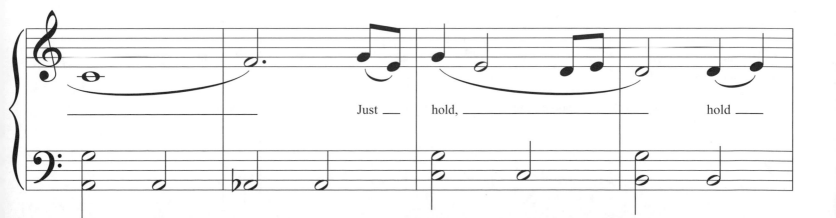

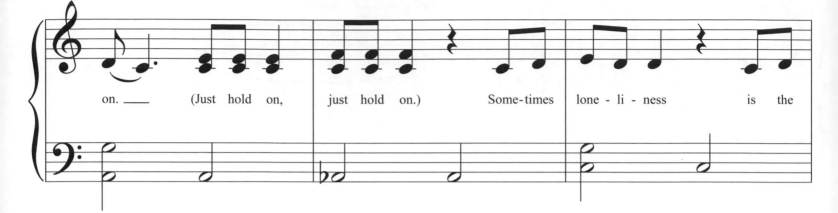

on. ____ (Just hold on, just hold on.) Some-times lone - li - ness is the

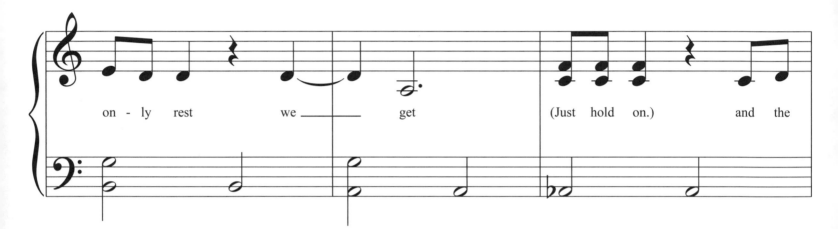

on - ly rest we ____ get (Just hold on.) and the

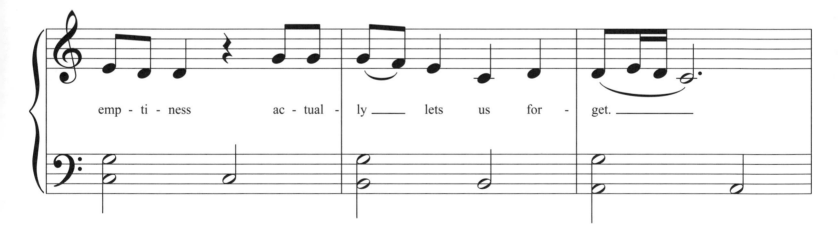

emp - ti - ness ac - tual - ly ____ lets us for - get. _____

(Just hold on.) Some-times for - give - ness is eas - i - est in

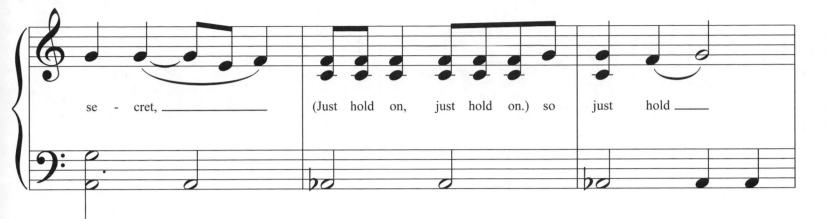

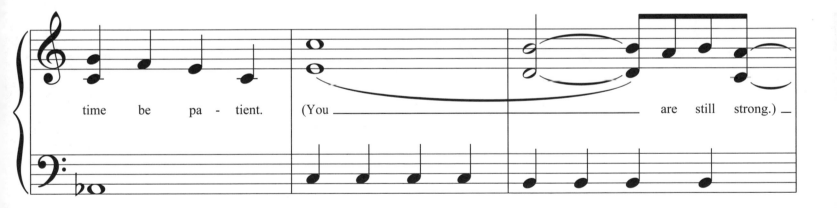

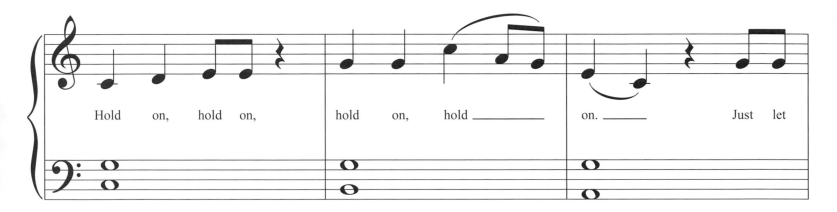

EASY ON ME

Words and Music by ADELE ADKINS
and GREG KURSTIN

Medium slow Ballad

There __ ain't no gold ____ in __ this riv- er _____ that I've been

wash - ing my hands in for - ev - er. I know there is hope _____ in __ these

wa - ters, ____ but I can't bring my-self ___ to swim when I am drown- ing in this

si - lence, ba - by. Let me in. _____ Go eas - y

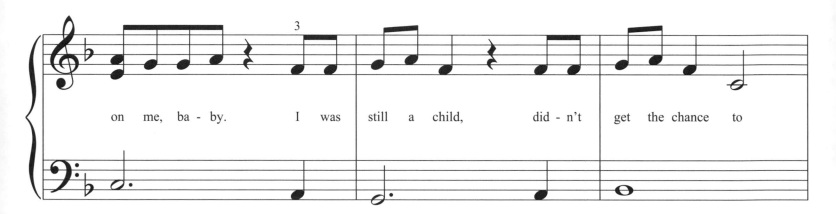

on me, ba - by. I was still a child, did - n't get the chance to

feel _____ the world a - round me. I had no time to choose __ what I

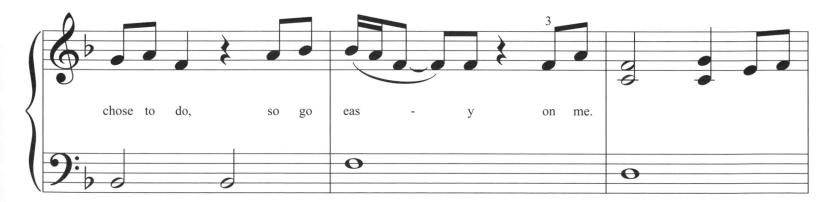

chose to do, so go eas - y on me.

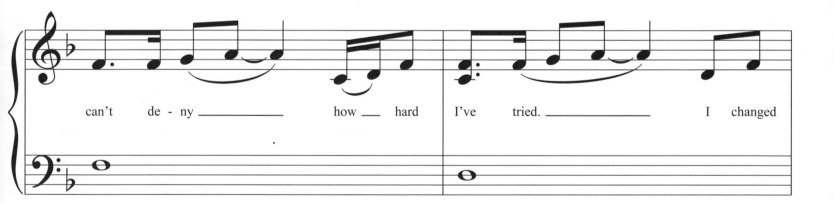

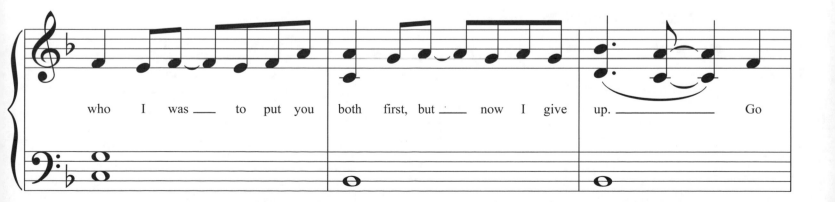

eas - y on me, ba - by. I was still a child, did - n't

get the chance to feel _____ the world a - round me. I had no

To Coda ⊕

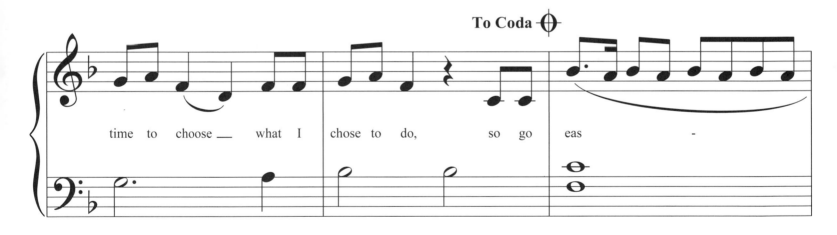

time to choose ___ what I chose to do, so go eas -

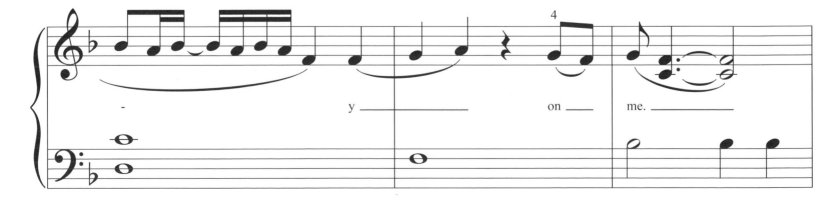

- y ___ on ___ me. ___

I had _____ good in - ten - tions _____ and the high - est

hopes, ___ but I know right now ___ it prob -'ly does - n't e - ven show. ___

D.S. al Coda

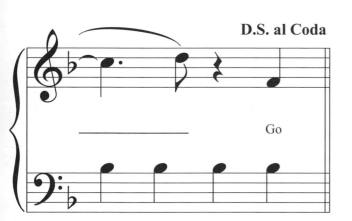

_____ Go

CODA

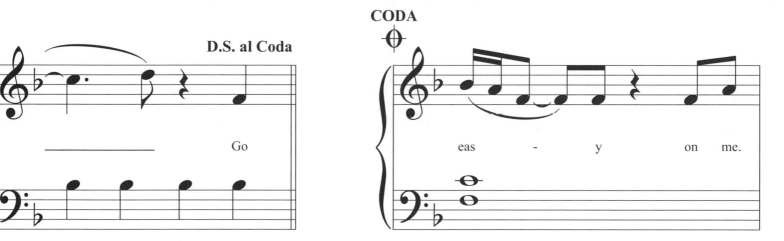

eas - y on me.

SEND MY LOVE
(To Your New Lover)

Words and Music by ADELE ADKINS,
MAX MARTIN and SHELLBACK

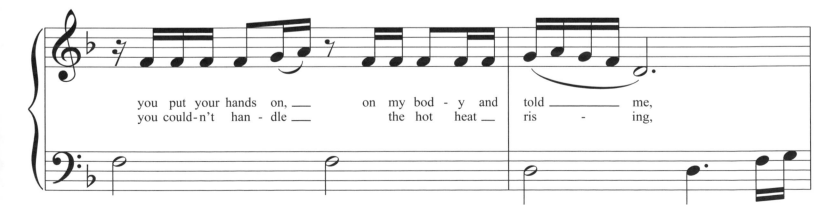

23

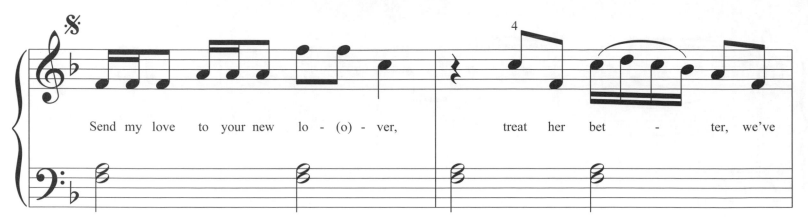

Send my love to your new lo - (o) - ver, treat her bet - ter, we've

got - ta let go of all of our ghosts, __ we both know we ain't kids no more. __

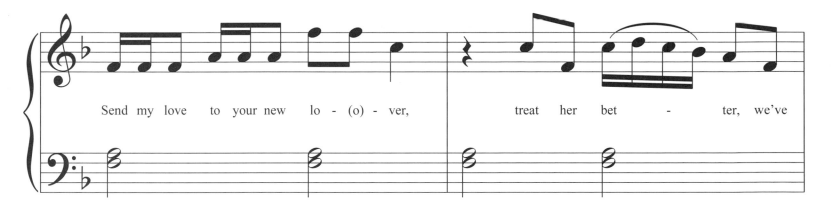

Send my love to your new lo - (o) - ver, treat her bet - ter, we've

To Coda ⊕

got - ta let go of all of our ghosts, __ we both know we ain't kids no more. __

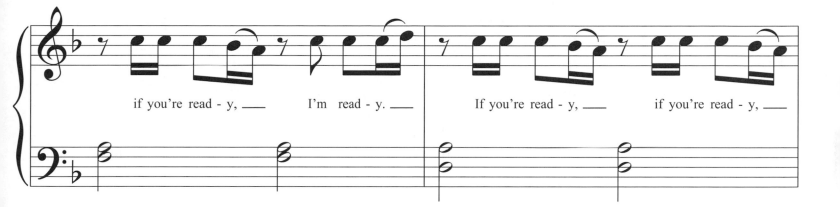

if you're read - y, ____ I'm read - y. ____ If you're read - y, ____ if you're read - y, ____

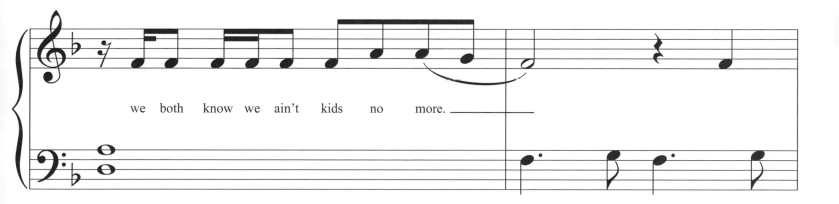

we both know we ain't kids no more. ____

No, ____ we ain't kids no more. ____

I'm giv - ing you ___ up,

D.S. al Coda

I've for - giv - en it ___ all, ___ you set me free.

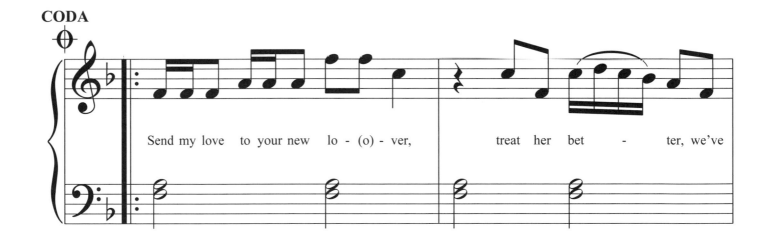

CODA

Send my love to your new lo - (o) - ver, treat her bet - ter, we've

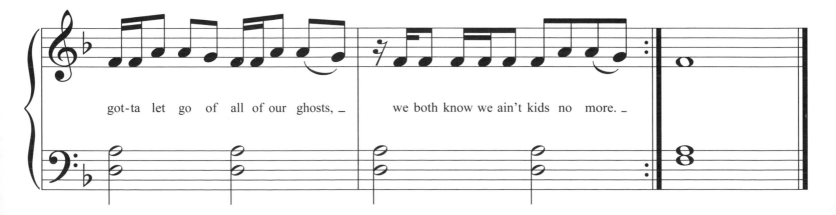

got-ta let go of all of our ghosts, _ we both know we ain't kids no more. _

HELLO

Words and Music by ADELE ADKINS
and GREG KURSTIN

Moderately

Hel - lo, it's

me. I was won - der - ing ___ if af - ter all these

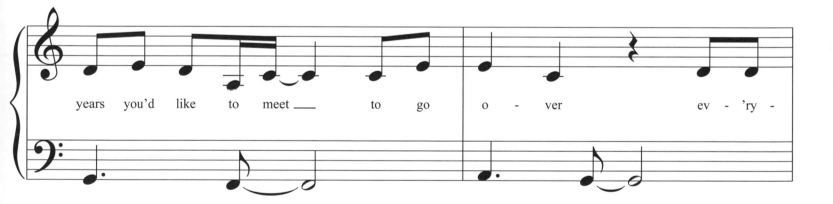

years you'd like to meet ___ to go o - ver ev - 'ry -

thing. ___ They say that time's sup - posed to heal you, but I ain't

done much heal - ing. Hel - lo,
lo,

can you hear me? I'm in
how are you? It's so

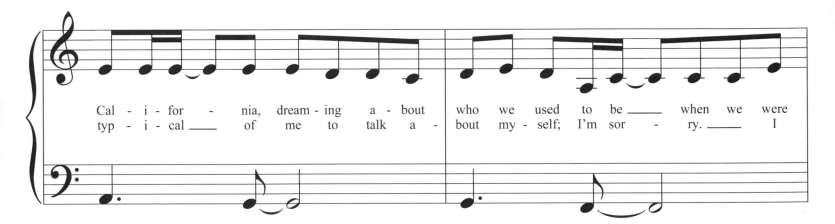

Cal - i - for - nia, dream-ing a - bout who we used to be ____ when we were
typ - i - cal ____ of me to talk a - bout my - self; I'm sor - ry. ____ I

young - er and that you're free. ____ I've for -
hope ____ free. well. ____ Did you

got - ten how it felt be - fore the world fell at our feet. There's such a
ev - er make it out of that town where noth - ing ev - er hap - pened? It's no

dif - f'rence   be -   tween ___ us, ___ and a   mil - li - on ___   miles. ___
se - cret   be that   both of us ___ are   run - ning out of   time. ___

Hel - lo from the oth - er side. _____   I

must have called a thou - sand times _____   to tell you ___

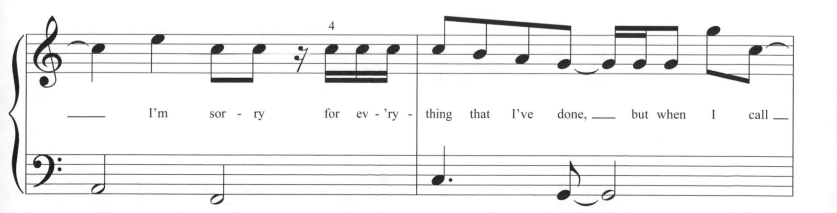

___ I'm sor - ry   for ev - 'ry - thing that I've done, ___ but when I call ___

you nev - er seem to be home. _____ Hel - lo from the out - side. _____

_____ At least I can say that I've tried _____ to tell you _____

_____ I'm sor - ry for break - ing your heart. _____ But it don't mat -

To Coda ⊕ 1.

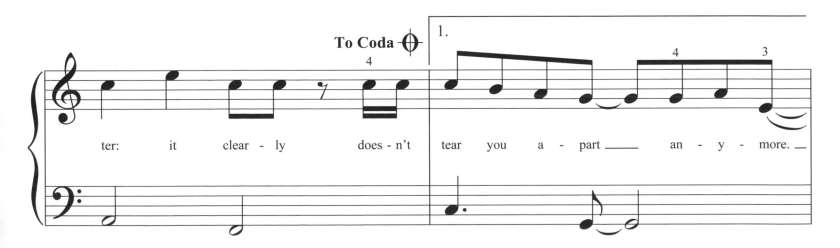

ter: it clear - ly does - n't tear you a - part _____ an - y - more. _____

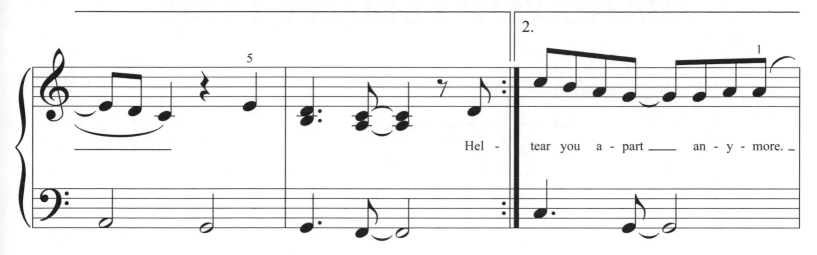

Hel - tear you a - part _____ an - y - more. _

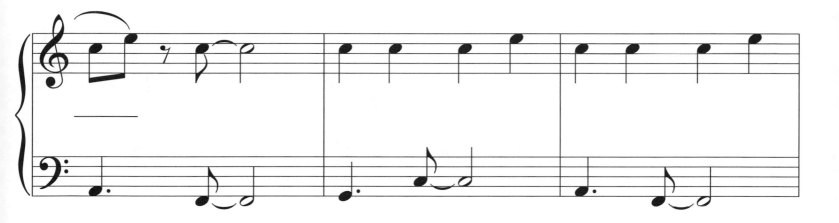

D.S. al Coda

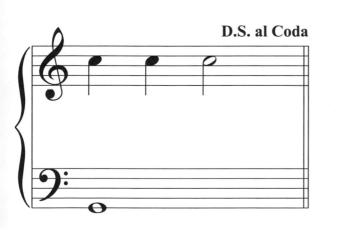

CODA

tear you a - part _____ an - y - more. _

MAKE YOU FEEL MY LOVE

Words and Music by
BOB DYLAN

Moderately slow

When the rain is blow-ing in your face, ____
When the eve-ning sha-dows and the stars ap - pear, ____

and the whole world is on your case, ____
and there is no one there to dry your tears, ____

I could of - fer you a warm em - brace _____
I could hold you for a mil - lion years _____

1.

to make you feel my love. _____
to make you feel my love. _____

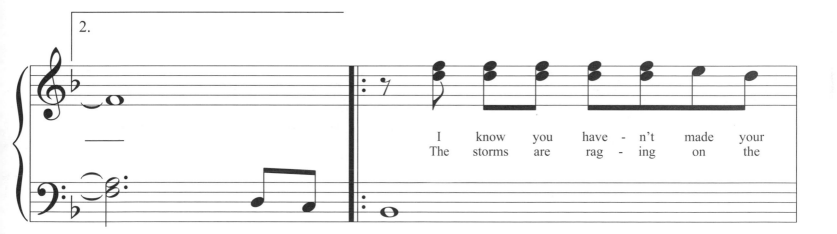

2.

I know you have - n't made your
The storms are rag - ing on the

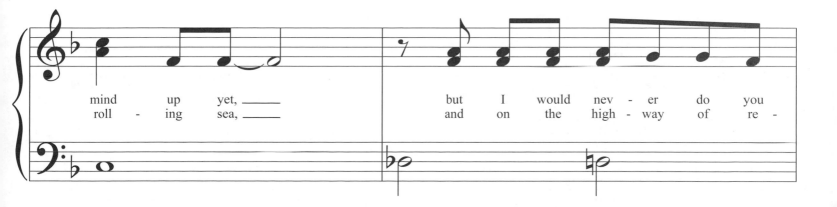

mind up yet, _____ but I would nev - er do you
roll - ing sea, _____ and on the high - way of re -

34

wrong.
gret

I've known it from the mo - ment
the winds of change are blow - ing

that we _____ met; _____
wild _____ and free; _____

no doubt in my mind where you be -
you ain't _____ seen noth - ing like me

long.
yet.

I could make you hap - py, make your
I'd go hun - gry, I'd go

black and blue, _____
dreams come true, _____

I'd go crawl - ing down the
noth - ing that _____ I _____

av - e - nue. _____
would - n't do; _____

Know there's noth - ing that I
go to the ends of the

1.

would - n't do _____
earth for you _____

to make you feel my love. _____

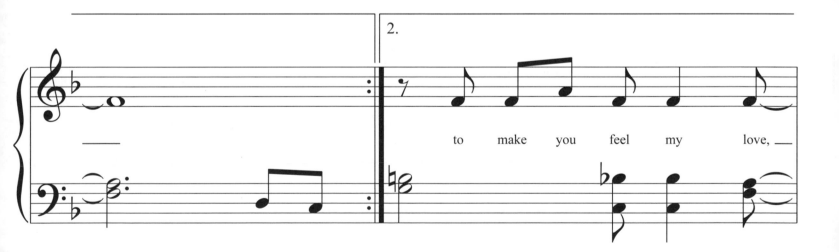

2.

to make you feel my love, _____

_____

rit.

to make you feel my love. _____

ROLLING IN THE DEEP

Words and Music by ADELE ADKINS
and PAUL EPWORTH

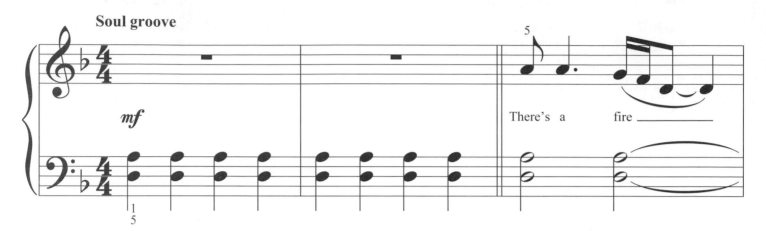

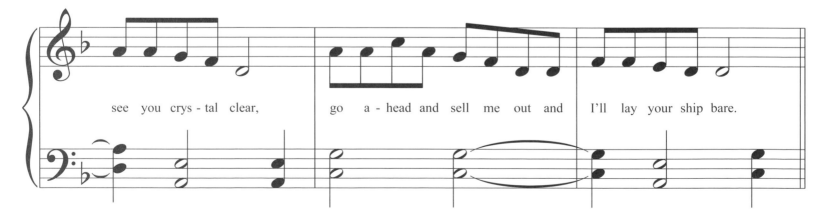

See how I'll __ leave with ev-e-ry piece of you,
Ba-by, I __ have no sto-ry to be told, but

don't un-der-es-ti-mate the
I've heard one on you and I'm

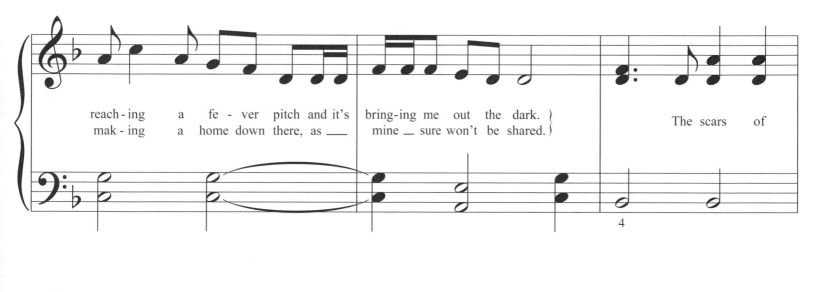

things that I will do.
gon-na make your head burn.

There's a fire ____
Think of me __ in the

start-ing in my ___ heart,
depths of your de - spair,

reach-ing a fe-ver pitch and it's
mak-ing a home down there, as __

bring-ing me out the dark.
mine __ sure won't be shared.

The scars of

your ___ love re-mind me of ____ us, they keep me think-ing that we al-most had it

all. The scars of your _____ love, they leave me breath - less, I can't help

feel - ing we could have had it all, _____ roll - ing in the

deep. _____ You had my heart in - side _____ of your hand, _____

_____ and you played ____ it _____ to the beat. _____

1.

2.

_____ We could have had it all, _____ roll - ing in the

deep. _____ You had my heart in - side _____ of your hand, __

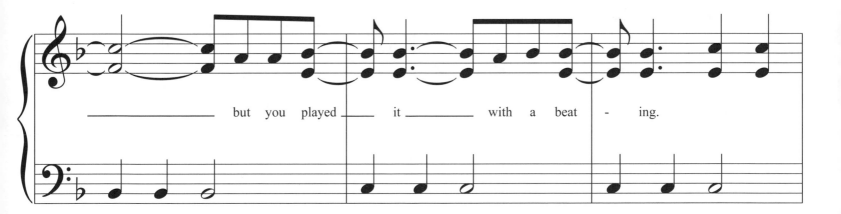

_____ but you played __ it _____ with a beat - ing.

Throw your soul ___ through ev - er - y o - pen door, count your bless - ings to

5

find what you look for. Turn my sor - row in - to treas-ured gold. You pay me back in kind and

reap just what you sow. ___ You're gon - na wish you ___ nev - er had met me, ___

tears are gon - na fall, ___ roll - ing in the deep. ___ You're gon - na wish you ___

nev - er had met me, ___ tears are gon - na fall. ___ We could have had it

all. _____ Roll - ing in the deep. _____

_____ You had my heart in - side _____ of your hand, _____ {and/but} you played _

1.

_____ it _____ to the beat. _____ We could have had it

2.

_____ it, you played _ it, you played _ it, you played _ it to the beat. _____

SET FIRE TO THE RAIN

Words and Music by ADELE ADKINS
and FRASER SMITH

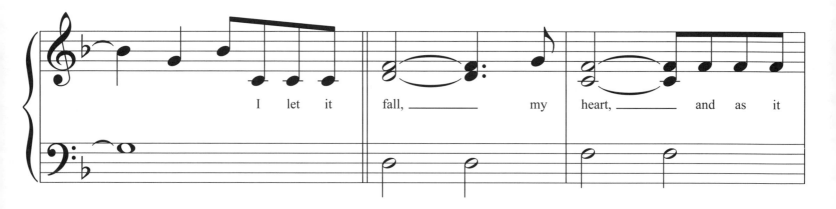

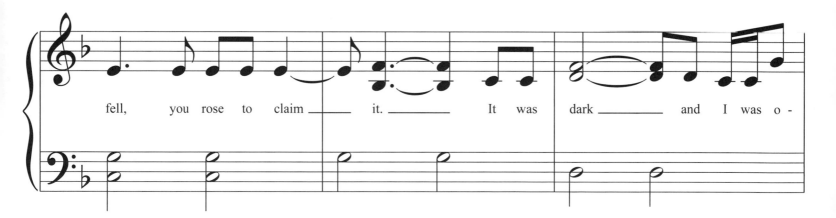

43

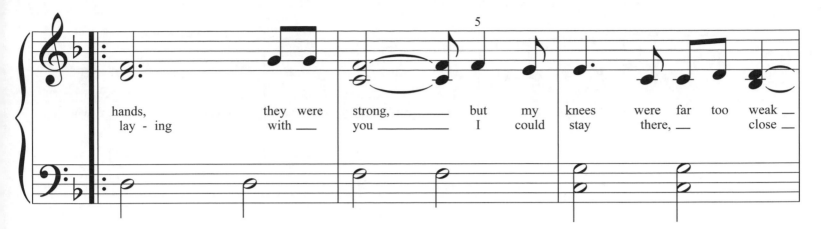

hands, they were strong, but my knees were far too weak
lay - ing with you I could stay there, close

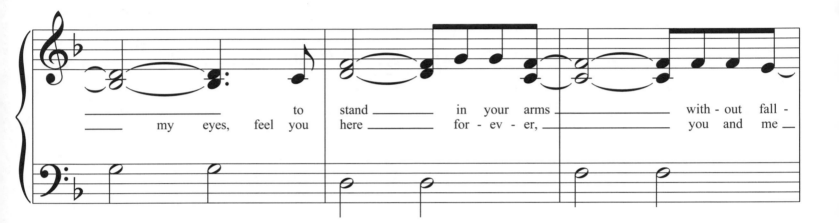

my eyes, feel you to stand in your arms with - out fall -
to - geth - er, noth - ing gets you and me

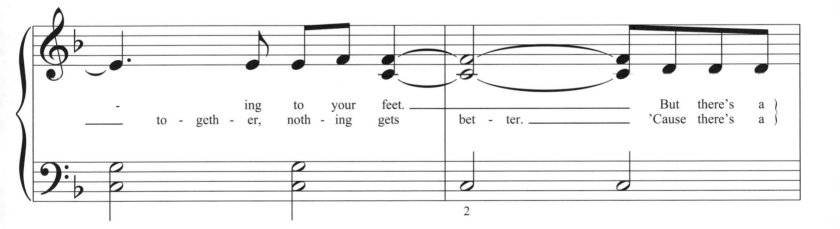

- ing to your feet. But there's a
to - geth - er, noth - ing gets bet - ter. 'Cause there's a

side to you that I nev - er knew, nev - er knew. All the things you'd say, they were

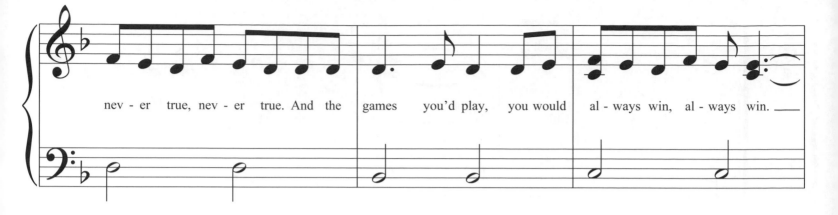

nev - er true, nev - er true. And the games you'd play, you would al - ways win, al - ways win.

But I set fire to the rain, watched it pour

as I touched your face. Well, it burned

while I cried, 'cause I heard it scream - ing out your

name, your name. _____ When _____ I set

fire _____ to the rain _____ and I threw us _____ in - to the flames. __

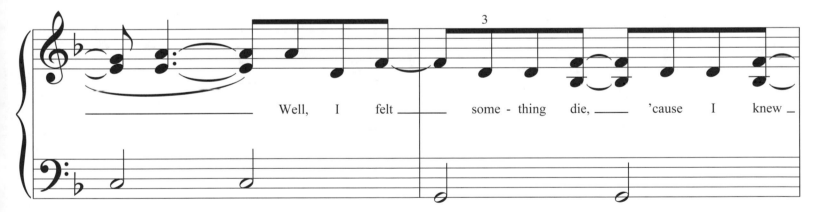

_____ Well, I felt _____ some - thing die, _____ 'cause I knew __

To Coda ⊕

_____ that, that _____ was the last time, _____ the last time. _____ Some-times I __

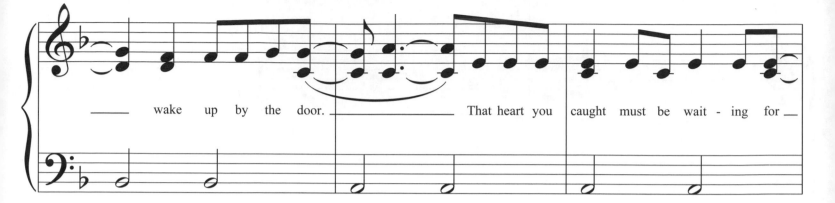

wake up by the door. _____ That heart you caught must be wait - ing for _____

her. _____ E - ven now, _____ when we're al - read - y o - ver, _____ I can't help _____

D.S. al Coda
(no repeat)

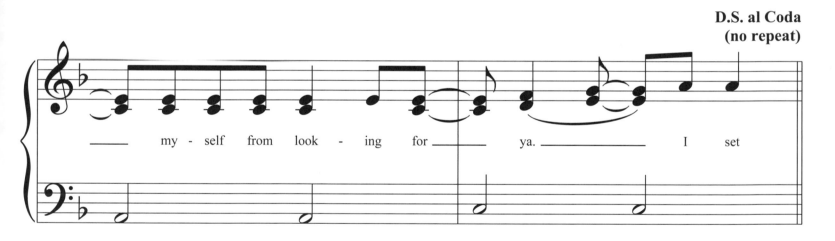

my - self from look - ing for _____ ya. _____ I set

CODA

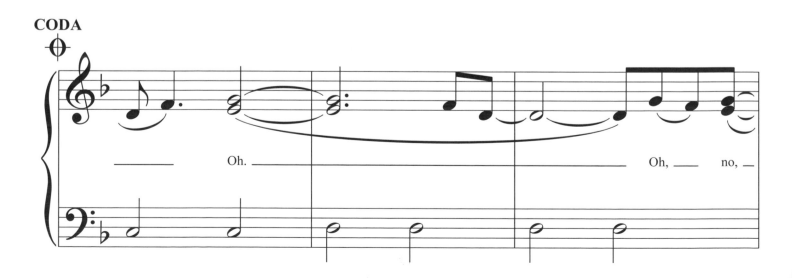

Oh. _____ Oh, ___ no, __

oh. _____ Let it burn. _____

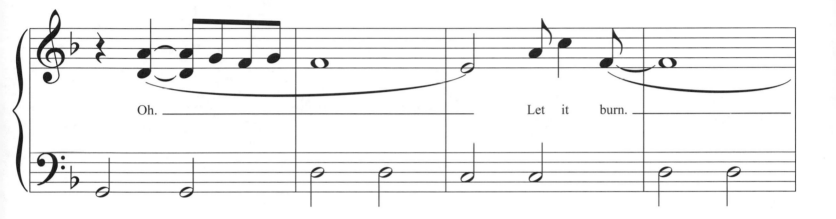

Oh. _____ Let it burn. _____

Let it burn. _____

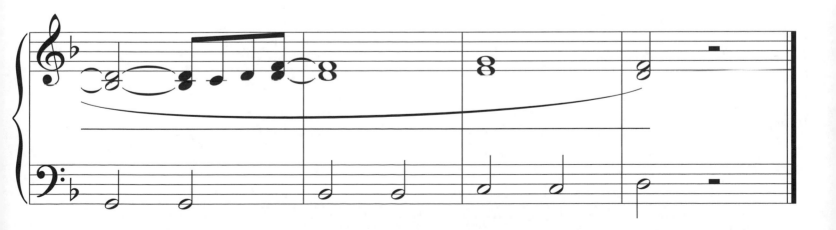

SKYFALL
from the Motion Picture SKYFALL

Words and Music by ADELE ADKINS
and PAUL EPWORTH

Slow, mysterious

Play 3 times

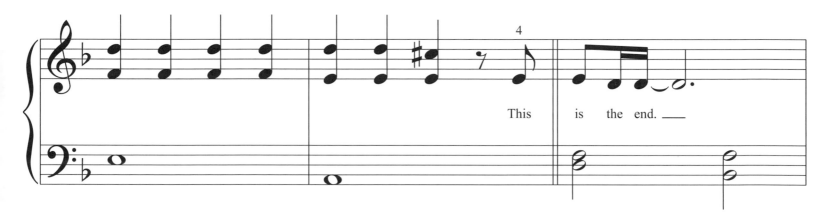

This is the end. ___

Hold your breath and count _____ to ten. Feel the earth

move and then _____ hear my heart burst a-

gain. _____ For this is the end. ___ I've drowned and dreamt this

mo - ment. _____ So o - ver - due ___ I owe them. _____

_____ Swept a - way, ___ I'm sto - len. _____ Let the

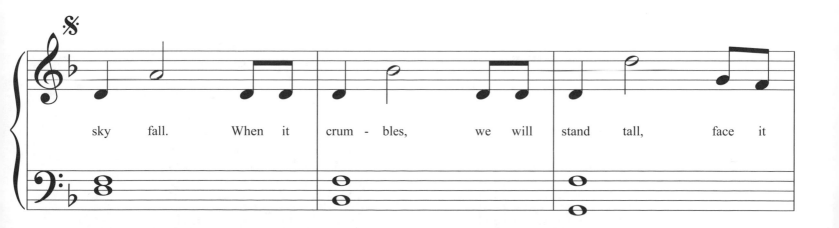

sky fall. When it crum - bles, we will stand tall, face it

50

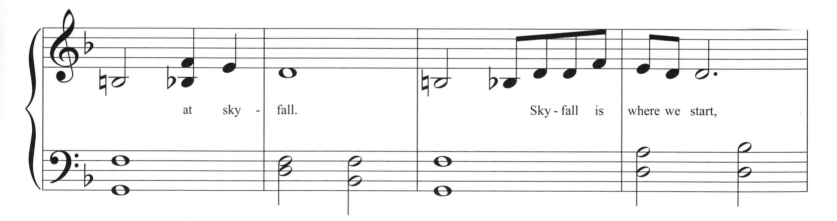

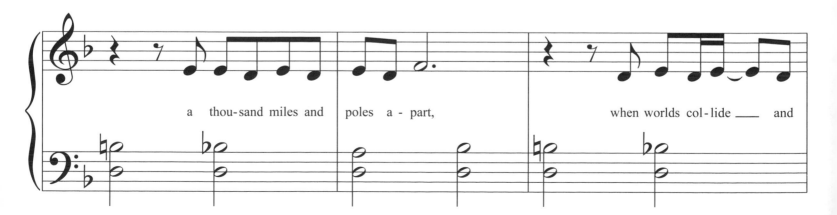

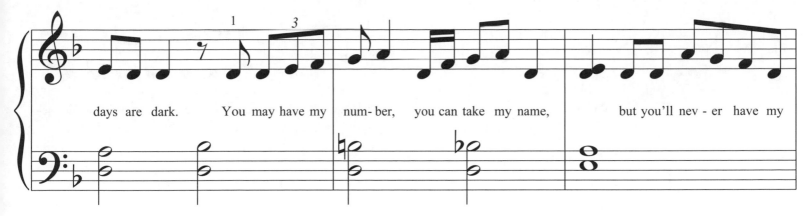

days are dark. You may have my num-ber, you can take my name, but you'll nev - er have my

D.S. al Coda

CODA

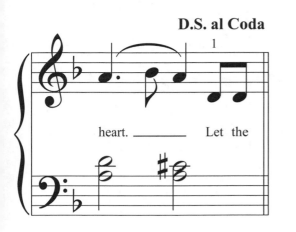

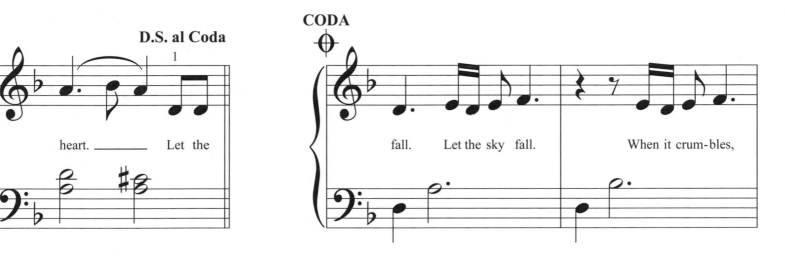

heart. _____ Let the

fall. Let the sky fall. When it crum-bles,

we will stand tall. Let the sky fall.

When it crum-bles, we will stand tall. Where you go,

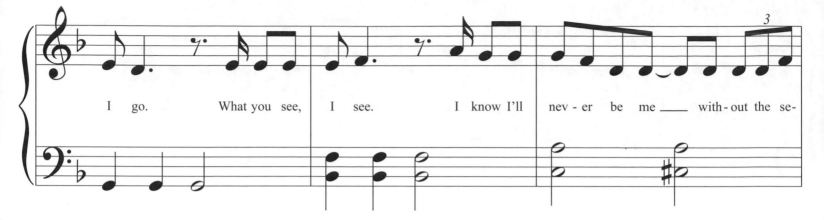

I go. What you see, I see. I know I'll nev-er be me ___ with-out the se-

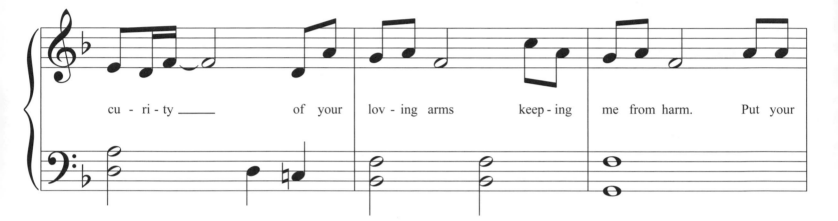

cu - ri - ty ___ of your lov - ing arms keep - ing me from harm. Put your

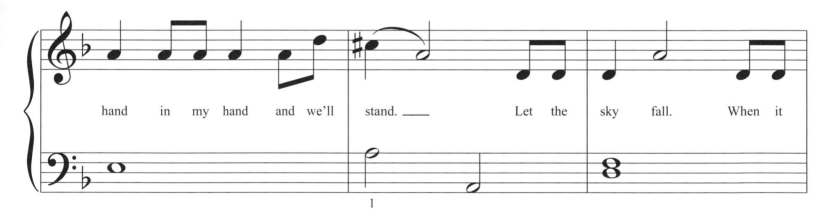

hand in my hand and we'll stand. ___ Let the sky fall. When it

crum - bles, we will stand tall, face it all to - geth - er. Let the

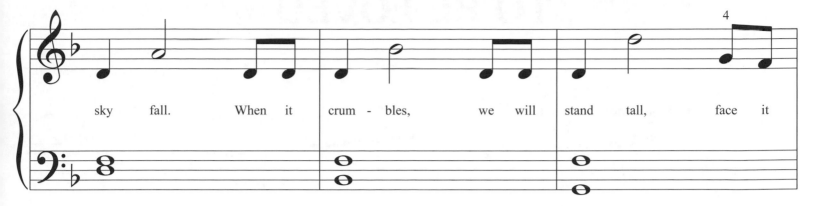

sky fall. When it crum - bles, we will stand tall, face it

all to - geth - er at sky - fall. Let the sky fall. _____

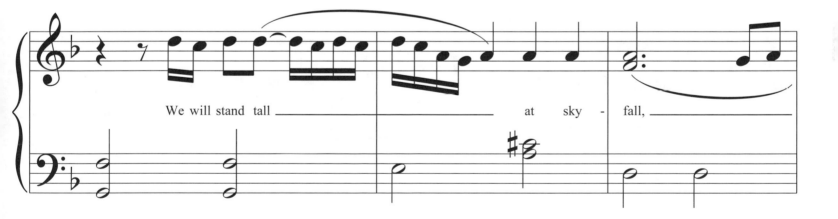

We will stand tall _____ at sky - fall, _____

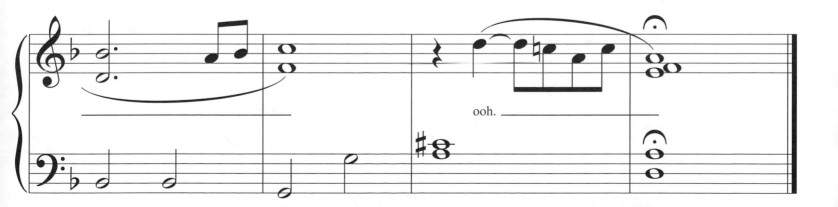

ooh. _____

TO BE LOVED

Words and Music by ADELE ADKINS
and TOBIAS JESSO JR.

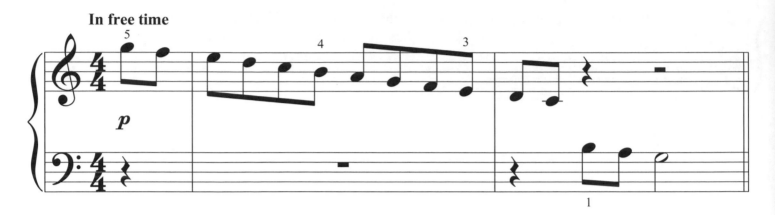

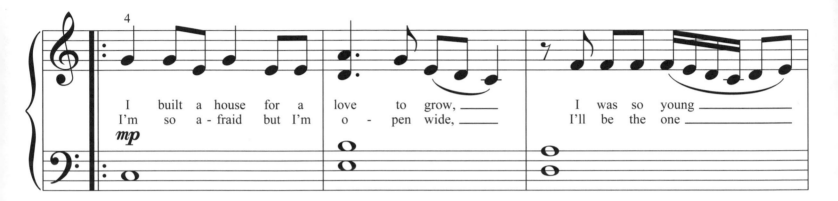

I built a house for a love to grow, ___ I was so young ___
I'm so a-fraid but I'm o - pen wide, ___ I'll be the one ___

that it was hard to know. I'm as lost now as I was back then,
to catch my-self this time. Trying to learn to lean in - to it all,

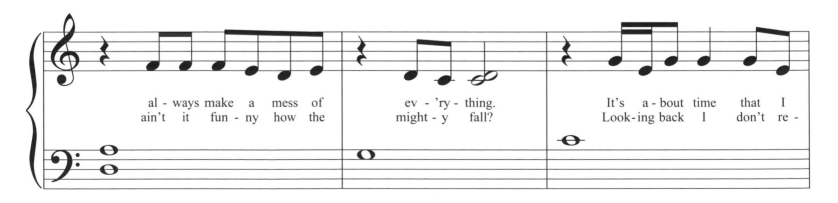

al - ways make a mess of ev - 'ry - thing. It's a-bout time that I
ain't it fun - ny how the might - y fall? Look-ing back I don't re -

face my-self, _____ all I do is bleed _____ in-to some-one else.
gret a thing, _____ I took some bad turns _____ that I'm own - ing.

Paint-ing walls with all my se - cret tears, fill-ing rooms with all my __
I'll stand still and let the storm pass by, keep my heart safe 'til the __

__ hopes and fears. } But oh, my, oh, _____ my, ___
__ time feels right. } *mf*

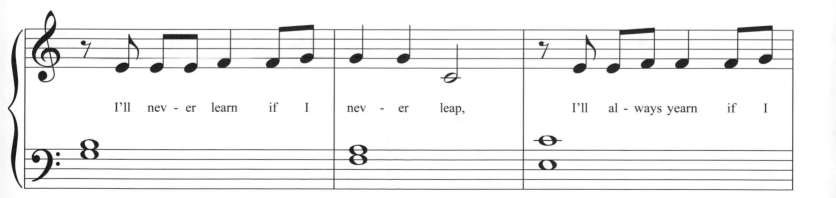

I'll nev - er learn if I nev - er leap, I'll al - ways yearn if I

nev - er speak. _____ To be loved and

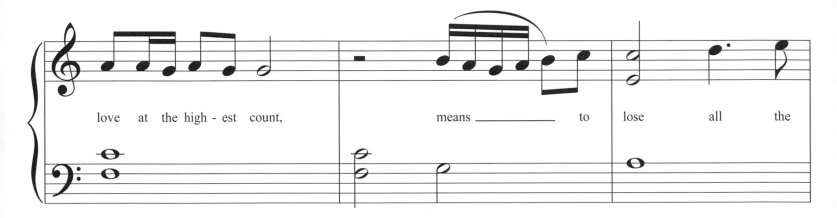

love at the high - est count, means _____ to lose all the

things I can't live with- out. Let it be known that I _____ will

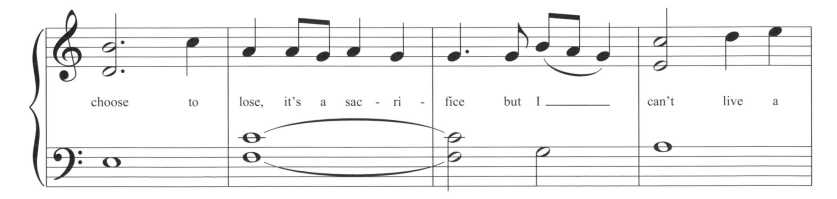

choose to lose, it's a sac - ri - fice but I _____ can't live a

To Coda ⊕ | 1.

lie. Let it be known,____ let it be known that I

tried. ____

2.

known that I cried _____ for you. E - ven start - ed

ly - ____ ing to ____ you, what a thing to do.

All be-cause I want-ed ___

CODA

known, let it be

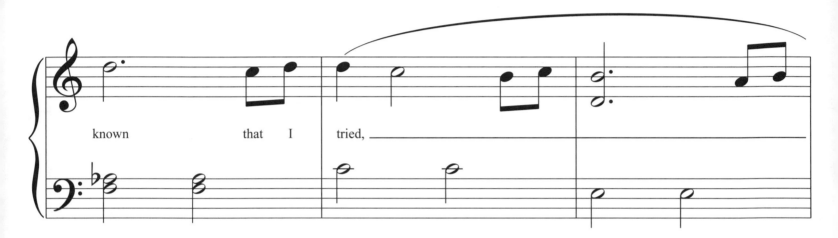

known that I tried, ___

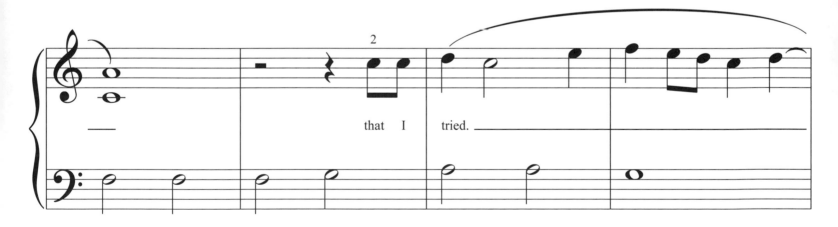

2

___ that I tried. ___

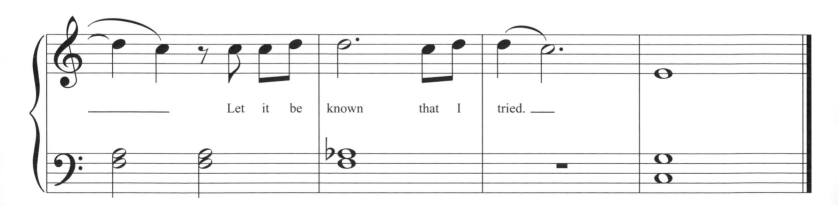

___ Let it be known that I tried. ___

SOMEONE LIKE YOU

Words and Music by ADELE ADKINS
and DAN WILSON

Piano Ballad

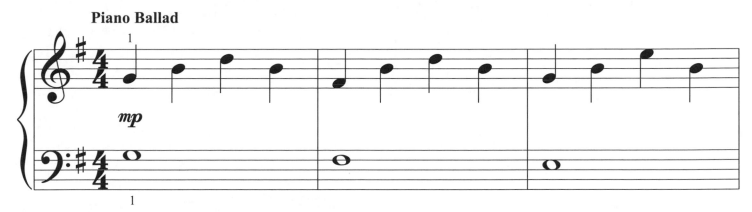

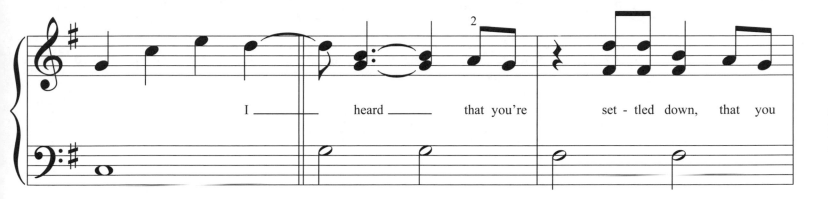

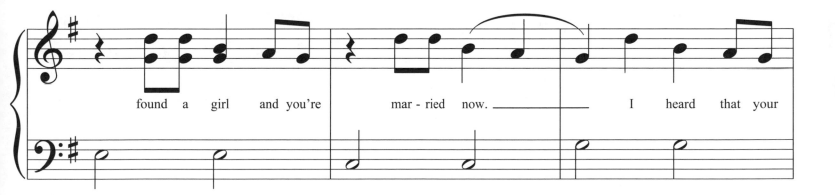

me, _____ it is - n't o - ver. _____

Nev - er mind, __ I'll find some - one like you. I wish

noth - ing but __ the best for you, too. Don't for - get me, I beg, I re -

mem - ber you said, "Some - times it lasts in love, but some - times it hurts in -

62

To Coda ⊕

stead."　　　　Some-times it　　lasts　in love,　but some-times it　hurts　in -

stead. _____　　　　　　　　You　know　how　the

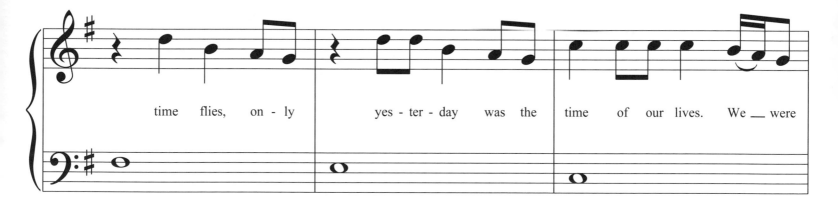

time　flies,　on - ly　　yes - ter - day　was the　　time　of　our　lives. We __ were

born and raised __ in a　　sum - mer　haze, __ bound　　by　the　sur - prise of our

63

CODA

stead. _____   Noth - ing com - pares,   no   wor - ries   or   cares,   re -

grets and mis - takes, they are   mem - o - ries   made.   Who would have known   how ____   bit - ter -

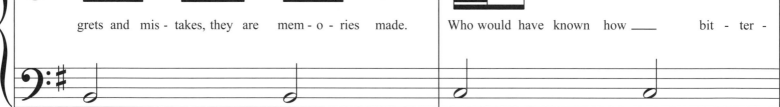

sweet ____ this would   taste?   Nev - er mind, __   I'll find   some - one like

you.   I   wish   noth - ing but ____ the   best   for

you,   too. Don't for - get me, I beg, I re - mem - ber you said, "Some-times it

1.

lasts   in love,   but some-times it   hurts   in - stead." _____

2.

stead." _____   Some-times it   lasts in love, but some-times it hurts in - stead. _____

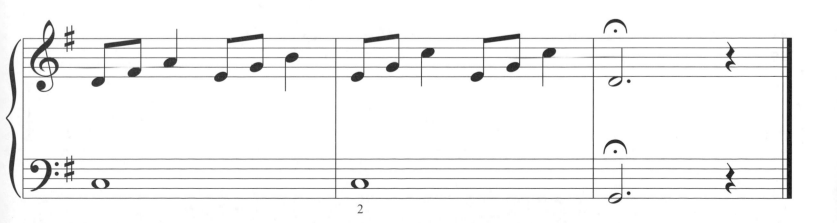

2

WHEN WE WERE YOUNG

Words and Music by ADELE ADKINS
and TOBIAS JESSO JR.

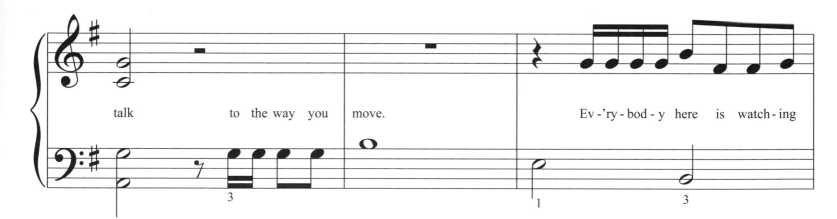

mov - ie, you sound like a song;
mov - ie, you still sound like a song;

my God, this re -

minds me of when we were young.

Let me

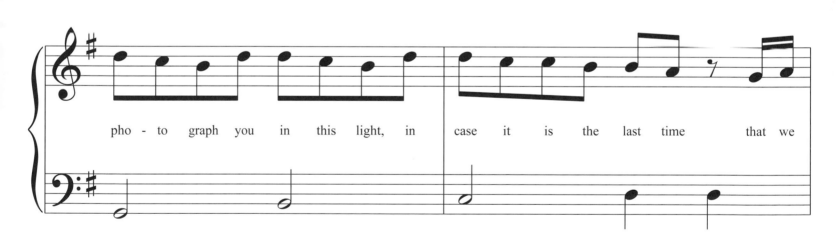

pho - to graph you in this light, in case it is the last time that we

might be ex - act - ly like we were be - fore we re - al - ized we were

hard   to win me there.   Ev - 'ry - thing just takes me back to when

you were there,   to when you were there.   And a   part of me keeps hold - ing on

just in case it has - n't gone. I guess   I still care.   Do

you still care?   It was just like a   mov - ie,   it was just like a

71

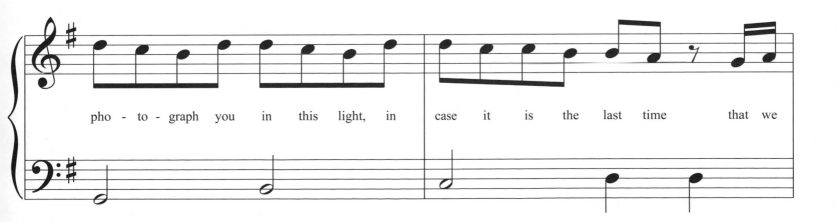

might be ex - act - ly like we were be - fore we re - al - ized we were

sad of get - ting old, _____ it made us rest - less. Oh, I'm so

mad at get - ting old, _____ it makes me reck - less. It was just like a

mov - ie, it was just like a song _____ when we were young.